Have you ever watched a raindrop wiggle down a windowpane? A rainy day can make you wonder. Where does rain come from? Where does it go? Follow a raindrop and find out.

The story of a raindrop begins here in the ocean. Rain falls out of clouds and into the ocean. The ocean holds billions and billions of raindrops — more than anyone could ever count.

But all of the rain doesn't stay in the ocean. The sun comes out and starts to shine. It heats up the water in the ocean.

Then something amazing happens.
Some of the water seems to disappear!

Heat from the sun has turned the
liquid water into water vapor. This change
is called evaporation.

Yoo hoo! Here I am.

Water vapor is a gas that goes into the air. You can't see the vapor or touch it, but it's all around you. The wind carries the water vapor up into the sky.

I'm back!

Way up high, the air is cold. The cold air turns the water vapor into tiny droplets of water. This is called condensation. The droplets float together to make a cloud.

Wisps and curls, heaps
and puffs — clouds come
in all shapes and sizes.
Which of these clouds
have you seen?

cirrus

cumulus

stratus

As more water vapor cools off,
more droplets form. Now the cloud
is packed full of water droplets.
The droplets begin to bump into
one another. They join and grow
bigger and bigger.

Soon, the droplets are too heavy to float in the air. They begin to fall from the thick, dark cloud. Look! It's raining!

Pit-pat-split-splat. The rain makes music on rooftops and puddles on sidewalks. It waters trees and grass and flowers. It fills rivers and lakes and oceans.

If it's very cold, the water droplets in clouds freeze into ice crystals. The crystals stick together to form snowflakes. Then snow falls instead of rain.

After a while, the rain stops and the sun peeks out. Can you guess what happens next? The sunshine heats up the water in puddles and rivers, lakes and oceans. It turns the rain back into water vapor.

The water vapor rises up into the sky again. This vapor will cool into droplets and form new clouds. In time, these clouds will make more rain. Then the whole cycle will begin again.

In fact, no new rain is ever made. The rain bouncing off your umbrella today has fallen to Earth billions of times before. Maybe it drizzled on the dinosaurs, or on George Washington's head!

And that same rain will fall to Earth billions of times again. It may splash against the window of your great-great-grandchildren, or shower down on people living far off in the future.

So, the next time you watch a raindrop wiggle down a windowpane, think of all the places it's been. Imagine all the places it will go! And remember that before too long, you just may see it again.